THE COASTS OF BRITAIN

THE
COASTS
OF
BRITAIN

John Freeman

Bison Books

Published by
Bison Books Ltd
176 Old Brompton Road
London SW5

ISBN 0-86124-217-3

Printed in Hong Kong

CONTENTS

This book celebrates all the varied aspects of the coast of Britain, and we welcome it.

At the National Trust, our concern is with the stretches of coast that are still undeveloped. Britain has one of the most varied and beautiful coastlines in the world. It has high cliffs, great beaches, lonely saltmarshes, intricate sand dunes. Its colours range from the white cliffs of Dover to the red rocks of Devon. Our coastlands offer beauty and open space which should be accessible to all. They are also places where people live and work, and where wild animals, plants and birds can survive.

450 miles to go
Twenty years ago, the National Trust launched Enterprise neptune as a fund to preserve the remaining 900 miles of unspoilt coastline around England, Wales and Northern Ireland. (Scotland has its own separate Trust).

Acquiring the next 450 miles is not a pipe-dream but a finite goal. But we need funds available for whenever unspoilt coastline comes on the market. Neptune rarely has time to raise the money for each piece of coast that is threatened.

For this reason, the National Trust is indeed grateful to W H Smith for making a contribution to Enterprise Neptune from the proceeds of each copy of "The Coasts of Britain" that is sold. There is a donation form on the back flap of the jacket for readers who may wish to make their own contribution.

With your help, we can ensure that the remaining stretches of unspoilt coastline stay a reality for future generations.

Left: Aberystwyth, Wales.
Below left: Weston-Super-Mare.
Below right: Blackpool.

THE PHYSICAL COAST

Britain's coast is made up of a myriad of changing physical forces. Although the days are long past since volcanoes and glaciers shaped and formed some of the fabulous strata that make up the country's cliffs and lowlands, the wind, rain and sea are still at work. While some areas are being eroded, others are in the process of being built up. There is a complex interweaving of waterways that make their way to the sea. It is here that fresh water from the rivers meets the salt water from the oceans, and the living organisms that lie buried in the estuaries, exposed by the shifting tides, provide food for many predatory birds and animals. Exotic plants and grasses grow here, as well as on the craggy heights and on seemingly tranquil sandy shores. Rocks and pools conceal a multitude of natural wonders to observe and explore. The pounding of the Atlantic Ocean, the North Sea, the English Channel and the Irish Sea have all played their part in shaping and protecting the intricate and varied edging of these islands, and their forces are still at work today.

The sea, wind and rain have played their part in sculpting the familiar shape of the British Isles, as much as glacial, volcanic and seismic movements. But as familiar as this coastal outline has become, it is still in the process of change every second of the day and night.

In view of the short period of time that we as human beings have existed it is sometimes difficult to grasp the timespan of the creation of the world. In later chapters of this book we will see how coastal towns have increased in size since Roman times; how industries that have prospered because of their coastal location have declined over the last two hundred years; how fishing in certain areas of Britain has not changed for generations, whereas the popularity of seaside holidays is a relatively recent phenomenon. Set against these aspects of Britain's coasts is the story of Britain as an island, a story that can be traced back for millions of years.

It was approximately 3000 million years ago that a succession of thick sediment layers was deposited on the ocean floor. These were hardened under compression and pushed upwards through the sea by movements within the bedrock of the earth. The earliest of these formations known in Britain are to be found in the north west of Scotland.

Previous page: Coverack beach, Cornwall.
Top left: Druidston Haven, St Bride's Bay, Wales.
Below: St Govans Head, Pembroke, South Wales.
Opposite: Eypemouth, Dorset.

Over millions of years this area has been
built up to an extent that would be
comparable with the Himalayas today,
and although subsequently eroded, it
still remains the highest and most
rugged region in Britain.

Following a sloping diagonal line
south from this point in Scotland we
arrive at the River Thames and the
South East of England. Until about 70
million years ago this area was
successively exposed and submerged by
the sea. It was not until about 250,000
years ago when the Northern
Hemisphere experienced one of the great
Ice Ages that the shape we recognise as
Britain was formed. The final part of this
transformation occurred when this ice
mass melted and water covered the land
that had joined the south east of Britain
to the continent, leaving the British Isles
as we know it today.

Although the length of Britain's
coastline is small compared with that of
other countries or continents, it is much
more variable than most. A wide range
of contrasting formations can be found,
from the soft chalk of the White Cliffs of
Dover to the rocky ruggedness of Cape
Wrath on the north west coast of
Scotland, from the granite headlands of
Cornwall to the marshlands of East
Anglia, and each area has a different
history. Within any one area however,
there can often be found some
anachronism that makes the
classification of Britain's coastline as a
whole an impossible task.

Situated facing St Bride's Bay in
South West Wales are the cliffs of
Druidston Haven *(page 10 top)*. These
rocks can only be reached when the tide
is out but even then they are kept
continually wet by rain water seeping
down from above. This gives them a
lacquered appearance which highlights
the subtlety of their colours, reminiscent
of camouflage. Standing out against this
background are limpets that attach
themselves to so much of this country's
rocky coastline with a tenacious
impregnability. Their stationary
appearance belies the fact that limpets
move at high tide when they search for
food. They live on forms of algae which
they scrape off rock surfaces. As the tide
recedes they return to their home base.

The limestone rocks at St Govans on
the Pembrokeshire coast *(page 10 below)*
are also only visible at low tide. In
contrast to Druidston Haven it is purely
the undercurrents of the changing tides
that have sculpted their sensuous folds.
These tides wear down the lines of
weakness in the rocks. Over thousands of
years these gullies become deeper as the
limestone is further eroded. However it
is the height of the tide as well as its
coming in and going out that can

Left: Mullion Cove, Cornwall.

13

produce a unique geological pattern. In different parts of the country the rise and fall of the tide may only be a few feet such as in East Anglia, whereas other areas may be subjected to a tidal height of 40 feet, as occurs in the Bristol Channel. As well as these regional variations the tide fluctuates from day to day depending on the time of the month.

These fluctuations are caused by the gravitational pull of the sun and moon and their relative position to the earth.

Left: Hartland Quay, North Devon.

Although it is smaller than the sun, the moon has a stronger influence on the oceans because it is nearer. As the moon circles the earth it causes a tidal bulge – high tide – directly beneath its path, and a corresponding bulge on the opposite side of the earth. Halfway between these bulges, the water is at its lowest, producing low tides. As the moon takes about 24¾ hours to circle the earth, there are two high tides a day with each successive day producing a high tide about 50 minutes later than the previous day. When the moon is new or full it is virtually in line with the sun. This produces the greatest gravitational pull and the highest tides, known as spring tides although they have nothing to do with that season. When the sun is at right angles to the moon – its first and third quarters – the gravitational pull is at its weakest and tides are produced that are called neap tides. Spring and neap tides occur every 14¾ days. At the time of the spring and autumn equinoxes in March and September, when the day and night are the same length, the ensuing spring tides produce the greatest tidal range.

At Eypemouth (pronounced 'Eep') on the Dorset coast *(Page 11)* it is rainwater more than the tide that is causing a change in the seascape. These cliffs, owned by the National Trust, are often subjected to land slippage. This is caused by water weakening the mutual bond that holds the rocks together. The cliffs are a rich melange of gault clay, greensand, marl and lias. Lias is a blue limestone rock of the Jurassic type and was formed 140-195 million years ago.

Below: Dunraven Bay, South Wales.

The shore going west from Eypemouth to Lyme Regis is a fossil finders paradise. One of the most spectacular discoveries was made in 1811 when a twelve year old local girl, Mary Ann Anning, found the first complete fossil of an Ichthyosaurus, a prehistoric marine reptile resembling a giant porpoise, measuring 21 feet in length. Later she found an almost complete specimen of a Nesiosaurus, and then the first Pterodactyl skeleton in Britain. So prolific were her finds that the Geological Society of London placed a memorial window in the parish church of Lyme Regis on her death in 1847.

Mullion Cove, Cornwall *(Pages 12-13)* is also owned and protected by the National Trust. The quays have been extensively repaired and together with the winch-house and fish cellars, the harbour has retained its old world charm. The cliffs that surround the cove are made of basaltic rock, that varies in colour from dark grey-blue to pale blue and from brown to black. The angle of the sun can also have an effect on their colour. Basalt is an igneous rock formed by being forced from the earth's core to the surface in a molten substance that cooled very quickly. This substance consisted of a fine mass of crystals –

augite, feldspar and olivine.

The rock formation at Hartland Quay, Devon *(Page 14)* and the one at Dunraven Bay, South Wales *(Pages 14-15)* are just two of the many rock patterns to be found around Britain's coast. The rocks at Hartland Quay are being worn along lines of weakness by the sea etching out fissures. As these fissures get larger the pounding of the incoming tide can cause a layer of rock to become displaced. As we can see, this exposes sectional views of a variety of rock patterns that typifies this wild length of coast.

The rocks that make up the cliffs at Dunraven Bay are from the same carboniferous period as those at Hartland Quay. The clearly defined layers of limestone and shale are an excellent example of bedding. Limestone is formed from the remains of coral and shellfish that have settled on what was once the seabed, while the shale is consolidated mud or clay. Walking above or below these cliffs can be

Left: Llanddwyn Bay, Anglesey.
Below: Claonaig, Kilbrannan Sound, Scotland.
Right: Stolfold, Bridgwater Bay, Somerset.

dangerous because of their crumbling nature. When the tide is out, further examples of weathered limestone rocks can be seen on the shore, many of which resemble huge surreal-looking waffles due to their honeycombed surface.

Helping to consolidate the sand-dunes at Llanddwyn Bay, Anglesey *(Page 16)* is a plant known as Marran grass. Although this is not the only plant to check the drift of sand it is the most common. Other varieties include sea crouch grass, which can also withstand being immersed in seawater, and sea sandwort. Marran grass is a deep-rooted plant which as it develops forms an intricate network of roots. It is these roots which stabilise the sand. As more sand gets blown towards the barrier of grass, so the plant pushes new shoots upwards and sideways. These shoots in time will fork and become part of the root system as yet more new shoots take their place. If the grass is destroyed, as once happened at Llanddwyn Bay, then nothing will stop the drift of sand. Here the grass was once used in a local industry for making ropes, nets and mats, but erosion became so severe that its cutting was stopped. There have been many occasions in the past when the sand was blown inland and buried fertile farmland, but now the dunes are owned by the Forestry Commission who have planted conifers along the four mile

stretch of the bay to prevent this.

In contrast to the wispy quality of the dunes at Llanddwyn Bay are the metamorphic rocks at Claonaig, overlooking Kilbrannan Sound in Scotland *(Page 17 bottom)*. Their sharpness and angularity gives them the appearance of cutting through the shoreline with a razor edge. Metamorphic rocks are formed out of igneous or sedimentary rocks but their character has been altered by intense pressure or heat. Metamorphic rocks include Lower Palaeozoic and Proterozoic types, which date from 500 to 1000 million years. The rocks from this period are mainly Schists and Gneisses. Schists are recognisable as fine-grained parallel layers of component minerals that have split into regular plates. Gneisses are coarsely-grained and the minerals are arranged in roughly parallel layers usually containing feldspar and sometimes quartz.

Stolford, Somerset *(Page 17 top)* is neither sand dune nor solid rock. Overlooking Stert Flats it is part of Bridgwater Bay Nature Reserve which extends for over 6000 acres. At low tide the sea recedes to reveal a huge expanse of dangerous mud which is deposited by the River Parrett. It is in estuaries like this that the freshwater from the rivers meets the saltwater of the sea. It is also

the meeting place for many different forms of wildlife that make up a rich and varied eco-system. The river water flows out into the estuary above the heavier saltwater. In between these two layers, and moving in either direction depending on the tide, is a layer of brackish water that is a combination of saltwater and freshwater. The rivers carry organic material that provides food for creatures living in the mudbanks. These include ragworms, lugworms and molluscs, which are in turn eaten by numerous fish like mullet and flounders, and birds such as gulls and waders.

When an estuary or bay is relatively sheltered and the tides are not too strong, salt marshes like the one at Pegwell Bay, Kent *(Page 21 top right)* can develop. These occur with the accumulation of mud and silt, brought

Previous page: Dunraven Bay, South Wales.
Below: Seven Sisters, East Sussex.
Opposite top left: Seascale, Cumbria.
Opposite top right: Pegwell Bay, Kent.
Opposite bottom left: Minsmere, Suffolk.
Opposite bottom right: Holy Island, Anglesey.

Top: West Loch Tarbert, Scotland.
Left: Eypemouth, Dorset.
Opposite: Hartland Quay, North Devon.

by the river and sea. If this build-up is allowed to continue to a point where the mud and silt remain above the level of neap high tides then certain plants will grow. These plants in turn will reduce the flow of the tide and silting up will further increase the height of the marsh. Moving inland, the marsh slopes progressively upwards and plant life becomes more abundant. At its lowest level only plants like green algae, sea purlane and eel grass grow, while further inland the attractively coloured sea lavender flourishes. At an even higher level sea manna grass is found which forms a turf as it gets thicker, that can be used for grazing cattle.

Whereas accretion occurs at places like Pegwell Bay, further along the south coast of England, the famous chalk cliffs of the Seven Sisters *(Page 20)* are subject to erosion by the sea. These cliffs were formed from sedimentary rocks between 65 and 140 million years ago, and are some of the youngest to be found on the coast. Sedimentary rocks, as their name suggests, are made from the sediment of seas that have since disappeared. As the waves pound against the base of the relatively soft chalk a notch is cut. As the notch encroaches deeper into the base of the cliff, the rock above collapses. Because the fallen chalk is quickly broken down by the waves a new notch is formed and the process repeats itself. It is because of the rapidity of this erosion that the Seven Sisters remain so remarkably sheer.

Another stretch of Britain's coast that has been subjected to extreme erosion is at Minsmere, Suffolk *(Page 21 bottom left)* where the sea has steadily moved inland. Just to the north of this beach is Dunwich which was a prosperous Norman town with a population of some 5000 people. In January 1326, a violent storm caused extensive flooding and destroyed much of the town. Its importance as a town diminished and the population began to drift away leaving the sea to make further inroads. Such were these inroads that between the late 16th and mid 18th centuries as much as 1000 feet of land and most of the remaining town were submerged.

With the coming of the railways, plans were drawn up to turn Seascale, Cumbria *(Page 21 top left)* into a north west resort town, but due to the instability of the boulder clay that form the cliffs the design never materialised. Boulder clay is a conglomerate of rock fragments bound by clay and is the residue left by a melting glacier. Today Seascale only consists of a couple of hotels and a few houses.

Because the clay is easily eroded, some areas of Seascale have to be protected. However, a far greater threat to the area than that from natural forces is the radioactive material that has contaminated the beaches and sea. This emanates from the nuclear reprocessing plant at Windscale further north along the coast.

The bay at Holy Island, Anglesey *(Page 21 bottom right)* reflects the tranquil and remote nature of this part of the coast. But as with all sandy beaches its existence is at the mercy of the weather and part or all of the beach could be removed by a storm. Sand is made up from a variety of materials, usually

Left: Old Harry Rocks, Dorset.
Below: Bedruthan Steps, Cornwall.

particles of shale, quartz, limestone and other rocks that have been worn down by the force of the waves. This material could be created from the surrounding debris, the result of wave erosion, or carried from other areas by the tides and currents. Sand is constantly shifting due to being covered by water at high tide and exposed to the wind at low tide, and therefore seaweed and other plants cannot survive on sandy beaches. Higher up the beach the rocky cliffs provide the necessary base for such fauna to cling to, as illustrated in the picture.

West Loch Tarbert *(Page 22 top)* is a sea loch on the west coast of Kintyre, Scotland. Lochs were originally ancient river valleys that have been cut deeper by glaciers. The deepest part of the loch

is usually the area where glacier movement down the valley was restricted in some way.

The rocks at Hartland Quay, Devon *(Page 23)* are being cut by the endless pounding of the waves that is characteristic of this part of the coast, whereas the clay cliffs at Eypemouth, Dorset *(Page 22 bottom left)* show clearly the erosion caused by water seeping down the cliff face.

Erosion by the sea has been responsible for changing the nature and formation of the coast, for example creating the chalk stacks known as Old Harry Rocks, Dorset *(Left)*, as well as the granite stacks of Bedruthan Steps, Cornwall *(Below)*. But the coast of Britain is also under threat from a variety of unnatural and unsavoury

forces. Oil spillages from huge supertankers or from North Sea Oil platforms result in marine pollution. As well as ruining beaches, the effect on wildlife can be fatal. Nuclear waste dumped in the Irish Sea from Windscale kills wildlife in addition to making bathing dangerous and contaminating fish. Overfishing has resulted in the decimation of certain fish stocks as well as the demise of small fishing communities. Land reclamation and barrages, such as the one proposed for the Severn Estuary, can alter the natural water flow and ecology. The dumping of industrial wastes and untreated sewage

in the sea contaminates fish and in turn, the birds that feed off them. Recreational use of beaches results in debris such as soft drink and beer cans and bottles which are not only unsightly but also a danger to wildlife. Every year an increasing amount of relatively unharmed coastline is lost in these ways.

There are many organisations however, working to save what is left, or to rehabilitate and subsequently protect what has been ruined. The National Trust started Enterprise Neptune in 1965. Its aim was to acquire 900 miles of unspoilt coast and protect it from damage and pollution. Since that time

Enterprise Neptune has reached the halfway point of this goal. Old Harry Rocks and Bedruthan Steps are part of this project. The National Trust has gone a long way towards rebuilding footpaths which were being eroded by the continual passage of visitors, and containing unsightly recreational development. Other organisations include the Royal Society for the Protection of Birds who manage several coastal reserves; the Nature Conservancy Council who are responsible for the conservation of flora, fauna, geological and geophysical features throughout Britain; and

Above: Loch Torridon, Scotland.
Right: St Govans Mead, Pembroke,
South Wales.

Greenpeace, who are well known for
their involvement in such issues as the
prevention of nuclear waste disposal,
whaling, and the killing of grey seals in
Scotland.

The north west coast of Scotland is the
home of some of the oldest rocks in
Britain. The mountains that skirt Upper
Loch Torridon *(Above)* are between 1500
and 3000 million years old and provide
some of the wildest and most spectacular
scenery in the Scottish highlands. The

majority of the rocks that make up these mountains are metamorphic and are from the period known as Early Precambrian. They are mainly gneisses and as well as being the oldest they are among the hardest and highest. Because of this height and hardness they have weathered erosion better than the softer, lower and chalky coasts of southern Britain.

In contrast, the limestone cliffs at St Govans Head, Wales *(Page 27)* are rapidly being broken down by the sea. This area of the coast is rich in superbly shaped stacks, bedding planes, faults and blow holes. Blow holes are depressions on the cliff tops tapering to a tube that leads to a sea cave below. At high tide when the waves crash into the caves, water is pushed at great pressure up the tube and appears on the cliff top as a water spout.

Along the Dorset coast there is an impressive stretch of shoreline full of sandy bays and coves, such as this one *(opposite)* which is flanked by the famous Durdle Door at one end and these elegant white cliffs at the other.

Ronachan Bay, on the west coast of Kintyre *(below)* is a haven for wildlife, especially the grey seal. These are the largest wild mammals in Britain and can be seen basking on off-shore reefs. Over recent years, controversy has surrounded the practice of culling the seals. Salmon fishermen complain that the seals deplete their fish stocks and ruin their nets as well as acting host to the parasitic codworm. But it is probably overfishing and pollution rather than the grey seal that has played the major part in depleting fish stocks.

The waves crashing on the rocks at Trevose Head, Cornwall *(bottom left)* or the menacing looking sea and sky surrounding Shieldaig Island, Scotland *(bottom right)* are reminders that although the more turbulent times of prehistoric Britain are past, the elements of sea, sun, wind and rain are still as active as ever.

Left: Durdle Door, Dorset.
Below: Ronachan Bay, Kintyre, Scotland.
Bottom left: Trevose Head, Cornwall.
Bottom right: Shieldaig Island, Scotland.

THE HOLIDAY COAST

For well over two hundred years the British people have flocked to the seaside. From the delights of children's bucket and spade holidays to the leisurely nature of retirement subtopia, the coastline of Britain has catered for holidaymakers of every class and condition. Although each year more and more of us take our holidays abroad, spending a day or a fortnight at the British seaside is still an extremely popular institution. Grand hotels and guesthouses still abound in spite of the growth of self-catering and camping holidays. Candyfloss and sun hats, ice cream and bingo, are just a few of the familiar characteristics of a holiday spent in resorts such as Blackpool, Margate, Clacton or Newquay. Sunshine in Britain may be rather erratic, but the popularity of wind-surfing on certain beaches compares favourably with many Mediterranean coasts. Away from the popular resorts, wild scenery and desolate bays wait to be discovered through cliff-top walks or gently sailing round Britain's inshore waters. On family holidays, many of these discoveries remain etched in children's minds forever.

For many people, going on holiday means 'getting away from it all.' This means getting away from the hustle and bustle of everyday working life, having time to relax and slow down. Some areas of coast obviously lend themselves more easily to this than others, such as Morar *(left)* on the west coast of Scotland. Those taking a holiday here can be sure of a peaceful time. The many bays provide safe anchorage for boats, and their white sands present a dramatic contrast to the darker colours of the highland background. A narrow ribbon of land separates the sea from Lock Morar, which at a depth of 1017 feet is the deepest lake in the British Isles.

Perched on the rocks lining the harbour wall at Mevagissey in Cornwall a young boy concentrates on his fishing rod *(below)*. Fishing is one of the country's most popular pursuits and one which requires relatively little financial outlay. Most parts of the coast and some lakes and rivers are accessible to anglers all the year round. As well as the satisfaction of catching fish, it provides for many a reason to sit peacefully reading or simply contemplating life. Furthermore it is a pastime that can prove equally fruitful on windy and rainy days, and dedicated fishermen sit with waterproofs and umbrellas oblivious to anything but the tension of their lines.

Weston-Super-Mare is a well-visited holiday resort but it is still quite possible to find a solitary place on the beach as this couple *(right)* have, since the sea recedes for more than a mile at low tide.

As we have seen, the sea recedes into the far distance at Weston-Super-Mare, and in recent years a section of the beach *(above)* has become a carpark at low tide. Nothing illustrates more clearly than this the changes that have occurred in modes of transport to the coast. The concept of the seaside holiday grew with the advent of the railways. Until then, coastal areas had remained largely inaccessible to urban populations, but as the rail network expanded, so did the size and number of seaside resorts. In the 19th century, Weston-Super-Mare changed from being little more than a fishing village to a thriving Victorian resort. Hotels and guest houses proliferated as it became easier to reach from Bristol and even further afield. It was not until the early part of this century that the British motorcar began to be manufactured and not until the mid-Fifties that the mode of mass transport started to drift away from the railways to the private car. Throughout the Sixties, the motorway and trunk road network grew. Railway lines to many small resorts were closed down as their profitability declined. Weston-Super-Mare however is still connected to the national motorway system via the M5. It is little more than a two hour drive away from densely populated areas such as Cardiff, Birmingham and London. Victorian and Edwardian town planners understandably made no allowance for cars which were then regarded with as much derision as the birth of steam had been. Consequently, accommodating the increasing number of cars is a continual problem and in the height of the summer, vehicles spill onto the beaches, which may solve parking problems but mars the beauty that a vast expanse of open sand can provide.

Travelling by rail meant arriving at a preordained destination. The advent of the motorcar however opened up another dimension in holidaymaking. Those fortunate enough to own a car could now be more flexible and spontaneous in their holiday plans. No longer was it necessary to go to a particular resort and stay in a hotel or guest house. With a car you could explore little known and undeveloped coasts, ill-served by public transport. This freedom was extended by the possibility of camping, or of towing a small caravan. Gradually, cars infiltrated places such as Pentewan in Cornwall *(left)* which had never been accessible by rail and had therefore never had many hotels or guest houses. Soon these were as populated in the summer season as the older resorts. This increase in mobility changed the holidaymaker into a tourist. New and bigger campsites and caravan parks have been built to accommodate this new flood of travellers. Cornwall in particular has become a very popular area to drive to, with its good beaches, pretty fishing villages and a reputation for a fair amount of sunshine.

Aldeburgh in Suffolk *(above)* remains one of the less accessible small resorts. It no longer has a rail connection nor a direct motorway link. Many Suffolk and Norfolk beaches stay relatively uncrowded, even during the peak season months of July and August. The lone figure of the young girl testing the water highlights the contrast between this resort and the mass of people at Pentewan. Accordingly, the seaside towns and villages along this stretch of coast such as Southwold and Walberswick remain quite sedate and unspoilt, while the long shingle beach around Dunwich attracts more fishermen than family beach dwellers.

Sadly, Britain is not blessed with a Mediterranean climate. If it is sunny today there is no guarantee that it will be sunny tomorrow. The long summer heatwaves that have occurred a few times over the last decade have surprised no-one more than the British people themselves, some of whom have been unable to deal with such continuous high temperatures. But in Britain the visible presence of sun in the sky does not ensure heat, and as the sunlight glistens on blue water, telltale flashes of white on the sea's surface betray the existence of strong winds. Consequently, on a seemingly sunny day on many of Britain's beaches there is no abundance

of semi-naked bodies soaking up the sun as one may see on the French Riviera. Instead, fully-clothed bodies lie dozing on towels or in deckchairs, women in sleeveless dresses and men with rolled up trousers. The intrepid holidaymaker is not deterred by gales of wind and lack of heat. The obvious solution is to bring along a windbreak, as this family has done at Margate *(above)*, which serves to protect everyone including the dogs. Others take advantage of the windbreaks and deckchairs already provided on Hastings beach *(left)*.

It is not just sunbathing and swimming that have attracted people to the coast, but also the belief that sea air is

good for your health. The seaside has traditionally been the place to convalesce after an illness. In the 19th century for example, one of the Brönte sisters, Anne, was sent from her home on the Yorkshire moors to the coast when she developed consumption, in the hope it would help improve her condition. Today health is still an important focus in many resorts, as shown by the numbers of convalescent homes found for instance in many south coast towns. For similar reasons of health and tranquillity, the coast has always attracted retired couples.

While the beaches of popular holiday resorts are crowded with families on a sunny summer day, many people are wandering through the endless little shops that line the seafront. Every possible accessory for holiday fun is on sale and repeated in shop after shop. The sun hats neatly stacked in the beachside shop at Weston-Super-Mare *(above left)* optimistically anticipating a hot day, can also be found in the 'Beach Goods' shop at Margate *(opposite top right)* which displays an almost identical set of wares. Other shops cater for the souvenir hunter, and their windows are crammed with gift ideas. Glass or china animals; plates, jugs and mugs gaily sporting 'Present From . . .' on the side; tricks and puzzles, naughty signs; plastic models; tea-towels – the most useful and useless things are there, cheap and cheerful for a ready market itching to spend its holiday money.

If you can't decide on a knick-knack to take home, what about some rock? Gone are the days when rock merely meant a long luminous pink-coated peppermint stick with a resort name printed in red all the way down the centre, whose letters distort into illegibility as you suck it into a sticky mess. Nowadays you can buy rock in a huge variety of colours and shapes. Apples, oranges, bananas, life-like plates of bacon and eggs, and large round lollipops decorated with funny faces are just a few of the delights offered on the rock stall at Margate *(opposite top left)*.

Sending postcards is another traditional holiday pastime, and is catered for by most seaside shops. The postcard rack outside this giftshop in Mevagissey *(above right)* covers the whole of the front wall. As well as sea-views and coastal landmarks, you can buy animal cards, art cards and those timeless saucy postcards. For those interested in social history, it is worthwhile to look at some of the antique shops in historic seaside towns like Whitby. In these you may discover boxes full of old sepia postcards, or early colour photographs looking brighter than true. Many have long since completed their journey through the postal system, and reading them confirms Britain's preoccupation with the weather. 'Dear Vera,' it says in faded brown ink on the back of an equally faded brown view of Yarmouth in 1929, 'Having a nice time, but the weather has not been good and Mother is feeling poorly.'

Because the British weather is so unreliable, a wealth of alternative entertainment is available in many resorts to fill the time on a grey or rainy day. Amusement arcades and fairground stalls and activities provide some of the essential seaside fun ingredients, and consume youthful energy, time and money. Clacton *(opposite below and next page)* is a resort within easy reach of the east side of London, and like similar resorts on the south east coast such as Margate and Southend, it is well endowed with fairgrounds, wax museums, fortune tellers and many other amusements to entertain the thousands of young people and families that flock there for weekends and holidays. The beaches and esplanades here are jam-packed with holidaymakers during the summer, who seem unperturbed by their close proximity, determined to have their share of seaside fun.

The seaside has inspired a variety of sports and pastimes to occupy people of all ages. The purchase of buckets and spades for the children can for example, provide active pleasure for all the family. Toddlers busy themselves digging holes or making lopsided heaps of sand. Older children build trenches, moats and dams to try to trap or block the incoming tide, or attempt to bury Uncle Ted up to his neck in sand. Parents however tend to involve themselves at a more sophisticated level. Constructing a life-like sandcastle, or some other sculpture takes time and concentration and can fill a whole morning or afternoon. Turreted towers flying different coloured flags, water-filled moats, bridges and intricate courtyards emerge from the cold damp sand. The essential wetness however, is perpetuated by the sea, and part of the attraction of building such fine works of art is the certain knowledge that within twelve hours there will be little trace left. Only a photograph, as of this castle at Westgate Bay, Kent *(right)* can permanently capture this transitory edifice.

Spontaneous beach games like catch, cricket and football are a familiar sight, while the sea is the place to paddle, swim or take out a boat. Only relatively recently have we begun to import more

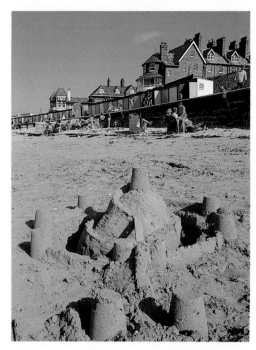

exotic sea activities like water-skiing, surfing and wind-surfing. Surfing demands a certain type of coast and sea, where the waves are large and have a sufficiently long run-in to make riding their crests a possibility. Some beaches in Cornwall, such as Watergate Bay *(below)* lend themselves easily to this

pursuit. For those doing it seriously, it involves quite an outlay in time and equipment. The carpark above Watergate Bay gets crowded with cars full of enthusiasts with boards and wetsuits of various styles and colours. The shops next to the beach offer for hire equipment to those wanting no more than to sample the challenge of the sea. Wind-surfers need calmer waters, but with enough wind to skim gently on the surface. Both kinds of surfing mean regular and usually involuntary dips in the sea, to the delight of onlookers. The advent of these activities are a welcome diversion for the more sedentary beach occupants, who get endless entertainment from lazily watching waterskiers doing figure of eights, surfers disappearing under waves, and wind-surfers climbing on and falling off their boards over and over again.

Other sorts of games have become associated with beach holidays. Putting and crazy golf for instance, can be enjoyed by all ages and levels of skill. Games like bowls however, as shown in this match at Eastbourne *(right)*, are taken more seriously and this dignified sport is usually enjoyed by an older age-group. White clothes and quiet concentration emphasises the precision with which each bowl is performed.

Messing about in boats is another popular activity, but one that requires a certain level of income to do seriously. Buying and maintaining a boat for pleasure is not cheap and the lines of boats berthed in Ramsgate harbour *(left)* reflect a high degree of investment. Many coastal resorts are now developing marinas to accommodate the increase in sailing as well as to exploit the commercial aspects. Harbour fees and club subscriptions have to be paid even for the smallest dinghy. A beginners boat like the Mirror Dinghy will cost about £300 secondhand. Such a dinghy is extremely versatile as you can sail it, row it, or speed it up with an outboard motor. From this, the enthusiast can progress through a myriad of boats costing many thousands of pounds. Learning to sail properly is very important as each year an increasing number of pleasure craft get into difficulties and have to be rescued by the lifeboat service. Many clubs belong to the Royal Yachting Association which runs courses on sailing.

For almost as long as people have been visiting the seaside, holidays have been recorded on celluloid. It was George Eastman, the founder of Kodak, who facilitated the movement towards collecting holiday memories with photographs which has never waned in popularity. It has always been common to find photographers earning their living on the seaside promenades, persuading people to pose with monkeys, or on donkeys, or wearing funny hats. It was Kodak who first brought cameras onto the mass market, and the early 'Brownie' and other box cameras took quite adequate if rather small pictures. Today there are enough cameras on sale to suit every type of skill and pocket. There is something very distinctive about holiday snaps, as captured in the family photo being taken at Morar Bay *(below)*. They don't have to produce expert results, it is enough that they provide shared memories of holiday enjoyment long after summer has gone and children grown up.

THE INDUSTRIAL COAST

The coast of Britain bears witness to a rich industrial past and a changing and somewhat uncertain future. Harbours like Dover, that were established in Roman times, have grown into huge passenger and vehicle thoroughfares to the continent, while Watchet in Somerset, pictured here, although still busy has retained its rural atmosphere. Many docks have had to adapt to new cargoes as changing market forces have diminished the importance of the local industries for which they were originally built. Shipbuilding once gave employment and prosperity to many towns but its worldwide decline has meant that many of the highly skilled workforce are now employed in new industries. The most important of these is the design and construction of oil drilling rigs and production platforms. North Sea oil has created other jobs in petro-chemicals with huge refineries now established in many parts of Britain. In contrast to these international industries are the smaller but equally important local occupations such as repairing fishing boats, running ferries and operating tugs.

The *Burmah Endeavour (left)* reflects the changing fortunes of both shipping and docks. This floating giant has been berthed at Southampton since April 1983 due to a worldwide slump in the demand for oil. Known as a ULCC – Ultra Large Crude Carrier – she was built in Taiwan and delivered to Burmah in 1977. With a length of 1241 feet, breadth of 221 feet, and a height of 244 feet from keel to top of mast, she weighs 457,841 tonnes. The main deck area is 5½ acres which would accommodate 2½ Wembley football pitches. But unless there is an upturn in trade, the *Burmah Endeavour* will be sold or sadly go to the scrap yard.

The fact that a ship of this size can remain so long at Southampton is an indication of the different traffic that the dock now handles. Berth 101 used to be the home of Union Castle for its Cape liners. The flagship of Union Castle was the *Windsor Castle*, and each week one of the liners would sail as another docked. Although associated with passengers, these ships were dual purpose and carried equally as much cargo. But times have changed and passengers are now carried by plane while goods have been put in container ships. Until this area of Southampton docks is redeveloped, ships like the *Burmah Endeavour* will continue to haunt its quayside.

Another dock that has seen the composition of its trade change is Swansea *(below)*, at the seaward end of the Severn estuary in South Wales. Coal, which was mined in the Swansea area as early as the 16th century, laid the foundations of a flourishing port. By 1700 up to a hundred ships could be waiting in Swansea Bay ready to load coal for export to England and Europe. The availability of easily-mined coal reserves close to the sea also stimulated local industrial development which in turn increased the trade through the port. Swansea continued to flourish as a port until the end of World War I, when, like an omen of the future, the first oil refinery in the United Kingdom was opened at Llandarcy near Swansea docks, by National Oil Refineries, now BP. Although substantial quantities of coal can still pass through the port, the amount handled has diminished, and it is the petrochemical industry that is the mainstay of its trade.

The scene at Mallaig on the west coast of Scotland *(right)* is typical of many small ports. Boatyards that build and repair smaller vessels are part of the industrial interweaving that sustains many small coastal communities. As well as being essential to fishermen, they are an important feature of the local economy.

Devonport, Plymouth is the home of a busy naval dockyard renowned throughout the world. Situated on a stretch of water known as the Hamoaze at the mouth of the Tamar river, it has been the site of a naval base since 1691. Now it is only one of three naval dockyards in the country, the other two being Portsmouth and Rosyth. After being extensively damaged in World War II Devonport dockyard has been repaired and enlarged. Today it employs nineteen thousand people and approximately seventeen thousand of these are civilians. This dockyard is now the largest ship-fitting and repair complex in Western Europe. Although primarily servicing ships of the Royal Navy, the dockyard also occasionally receives NATO vessels.

The huge grey building looking like an aircraft hangar by the waterside is the frigate complex which was opened in 1977. As this area is covered, work can continue uninterrupted around the clock enabling frigates to be refitted extremely quickly and efficiently. The ship outside the complex is HMS *Arrow*, a type 21 frigate. She weighs 2860 tonnes and is 384 feet in length. As well as carrying torpedoes she is fitted with Sea Cat and Exocet missile systems and has a landing pad for a Lynx helicopter. Rosyth in Scotland is Britain's main submarine base and the only one capable of handling Polaris, but Devonport too is an operational base for nuclear-powered submarines. It has a Submarine Refit Complex (SRC) and is designed to cater for the new Swiftsure and Trafalgar class submarines. All this activity makes the dockyard at Devonport very important to the local economy, not just by virtue of the number of people employed but as an attraction to tourists.

Equally important to local industry are the tugs that manoeuvre the ships. The two pictured *(left)* have lost their 'tug boat Annie' appearance and have become the most familiar type of tug to be seen throughout Britain's dockyards. Despite the decline in shipping and the increased manoeuvreability of modern vessels, tugs have not outlived their main function and indeed are used for many other purposes. These two were built in 1962, and each has a crew of five, consisting of Skipper, Mate, Engineer and two deckhands. As well as assisting ships to dock, tugs may be used for coastal towing, going to the aid of vessels caught in bad weather, and also for spraying oil-polluted waters.

The Torpoint Ferry *(right)* makes its contribution to Devonport as a means of taking tourists and their cars across to

Cornwall and back. As an alternative to the Tamar Bridge, it also carries goods vehicles, coaches, and people travelling to work, many of whom work in the dockyard. The first Torpoint Ferry was inaugurated in 1791 and consisted of rowing and sailing boats. Their efficiency left much to be desired as they were at the mercy of the wind and tide. The three ferries that run today's service work by means of chains that span the estuary. There is one chain on each side of the ferry. These pass through a mechanism that propels the ferry from one bank to the other and stops the ferry from drifting. When the ferry is in at either shoreline the chains lie at the bottom of the estuary to enable other shipping to pass unhindered.

Dover harbour *(following page)* has been a cross-channel port for more than two thousands years. The present harbour is the eleventh to be constructed since Roman times. The Dover Harbour Board was established by James I in 1606 to administer, maintain and improve the harbour which resulted in Dover becoming Britain's premier seaport and the only one of the original Cinque Ports to remain operational today. In 1953, two drive-on, drive-off ferry berths were opened at the Eastern Docks. There are now nine, including a specialist freight berth. Further developments include a Hoverport at the Western Docks in 1978, and the operation of the Jetfoil service and its terminal in 1981. Together, these facilities handle nearly 2½ million passenger and freight vehicles per year to five Continental ports making Dover Britain's busiest ferry port.

HARBOUR BOARD · EASTERN DOCKS

BOULOGNE		BOULOGNE		ARRIVALS HALL
CALAIS		CALAIS		
DUNKIRK	FERRIES	DUNKIRK	FERRIES	AA ENQUIRIES
OSTEND		OSTEND		
ZEEBRUGGE		ZEEBRUGGE		

Booking Hall

STOP STOP

The Tyne on the north east coast of England has always been synonymous with shipbuilding and the Swan Hunter shipyard *(below)* is one of the oldest. Many of the ships that it builds are for the Royal Navy like the one pictured here, HMS *Illustrious*. Other ships bearing famous names like HMS *King George V*, HMS *Kelly* (captained by Lord Mountbatten in World War II) and HMS *Ark Royal*, were also constructed here. With the worldwide slump in shipbuilding all British yards are finding it hard to survive and the Tyne is no exception despite its traditionally skilled workforce.

It is to be hoped that shipbuilding will not suffer a similar fate to the Botallack Mine, Cornwall *(right)* which illustrates how a once prosperous industry can become a relic of time. Tin was mined in Cornwall for hundreds of years but deep shafts were impossible to sink because of flooding. It was not until the 18th century when Thomas Newcomen invented a steam engine that would pump water from the workings, that the industry really flourished. Later, Richard Trevithick developed the engine further and it became known as the Cornish beam engine which enabled mines to go down over 3000 feet. This area was also important for copper and by the 19th century more than 75 per cent of the world's copper came from Cornwall and more than 100 mines were working within a small area of the county. Sadly this mining industry had collapsed by the end of the century due to cheap imported tin and copper. Although there are still a few mines working, the old ruined engine houses scattered over Cornwall are a grim reminder of the power of international market forces.

Richborough Power Station, Kent *(left)* takes its name from the nearby Roman fort, built about AD 285. Building the power station began in 1958 and was completed by 1963. Its three huge cooling towers loom ominously over Pegwell Bay. Originally it was designed to burn coal and was to be a major outlet for the neighbouring Kent coalfield. Between 1962 and 1971 it burnt roughly 3,200,000 tons of coal. Unfortunately, due to a change in national fuel policy it was converted to oil in 1971, and only two years later had to contend with the first world oil crisis. The outcome of this is that the still productive local coal mines are now threatened with closure.

Probably the most controversial power station in Britain is Calder Hall on the Cumbrian coast *(below)*, which is part of a nuclear reprocessing complex known as Windscale. Its name was recently changed to Sellafield. Many people believe this was done to disassociate it from a series of accidents when discharged radioactive material polluted the sea and seashore. Sellafield supplies very little electricity to the national grid, its main function is to reprocess spent nuclear fuel from nearly all the industrial countries of the West, and Japan. Every day, radioactive waste from the reprocessing plant is pumped into the Irish Sea, causing concern among environmental groups and local inhabitants. But while Sellafield is the focus of controversial attention for Britain's nuclear industry, there are other areas that give cause for concern in protecting and preserving the British coastline. All dumping of toxic wastes, raw sewage, domestic and industrial wastes, oil spillages are a threat to Britain's maritime environment. Much is being done to draw public attention to this by groups such as Greenpeace, while the National Trust's 'Enterprise Neptune' is in the process of acquiring 900 miles of unspoilt coastline in order to preserve it as such.

Britain's industrial revolution owes much of its momentum to the railways. The ability of steam trains to carry heavy and bulky goods, as well as people, gave access to areas of the country hitherto sparsely populated, if not deserted. Arnside in Cumbria consisted of a few houses and an inn but following the building of the viaduct across the Kent Estuary *(above)* in 1857, it grew into a small town. Railways dramatically changed the appearance of Britain's coast. Fishing villages prospered as trains could take their catches to urban markets in a matter of hours. Docks flourished since railway lines came right to the quayside from the factories and mills inland. Coastal resorts grew as the Victorians took to the health-giving qualities of sea-bathing. Arnside was just such a resort and since those days has found favour with sailing. A boat building industry developed and brought new employment. It also became a haven for the walker and ornithologist as the mudflats provide nesting for nearly every sea bird known in Britain. Although the importance of the railways has declined, Arnside is still a busy resort.

Angle, South Wales *(opposite bottom)* was chosen as the site for an oil refinery, built in 1964, because it has a natural deepwater harbour capable of accommodating supertankers. The refined petroleum products are exported all over Britain and Europe. Across the estuary of Milford Haven, next to the town of the same name, stands another refinery. From the economic point of view, the oil boom has come at the right time for this area, replacing its declining fishing industry. But any financial gains have to be set against the ugliness this brings to the lovely Pembrokeshire coastline and the constant threat of pollution.

The slag heap at the Moss Bay Iron and Steel Works at Workington, Cumbria *(below)* is another monument to a prosperous industrial past. Iron and steel working flourished in this part of the world because of the high quality hermatite iron ore being used to produce the iron. It was in 1856 that Henry Bessemer invented a new method to convert pig iron into steel, subsequently known as the Bessemer steel-making process. It was not long before every maker of Bessemer steel in Britain came to this area for their pig iron, a tradition that was to continue for almost a hundred years. This process is now redundant, the slag is being cleared and the area is to be landscaped back to its natural beauty.

Peterhead, on the east coast of Scotland *(right)* developed as a whaling port and between 1793 and 1893 it was even more important than Aberdeen. But failure to keep up with modern whaling methods or to embark on longer voyages such as to the Arctic regions led to the industry's decline and extinction. Since the mid 19th century it has become a major fishing port and its large harbour is the home of some 400 fishing boats. In the last few years however, Peterhead has established itself as a base for the North Sea oil industry. Consequently many new manufacturing industries have flourished and supply vessels take their products out to the rigs and production platforms in the North Sea waters. Just up the coast is situated the gigantic terminal at St Fergus, which takes the gas from the Frigg and Brent fields.

The exploration of oil in the North Sea has brought prosperity to many areas of Scotland as well as to the United Kingdom as a whole. This British Petroleum oil production platform *(opposite)* is in the North Cormorant field off the north east coast of Shetland. The weather in the North Sea and this area in particular can be treacherous and the platforms may have to withstand winds of 120 mph and waves up to 100 feet. Many rigs and platforms are built at deep water sites such as Nigg Bay on the Cromarty Firth or Loch Kishorn on the

west coast, so that they may be floated and towed out to their positions in the North Sea

Once the production platform is in position, the oil is forced out of the sedimentary rock that is thousands of feet below the seabed. In some cases it is pumped to a floating mooring point and loaded into tankers for distribution to the refineries. The oil from the North Cormorant field flows into the Brent system pipeline that goes to Sullom Voe

in the Shetlands, and here it is again loaded into tankers. Gas is separated from the oil and piped to the gas terminal at St Fergus. Other terminals are at Flotta in the Orkneys, Cruden Bay, Grangemouth and Shandwick on the Scottish mainland.

Each production platform or drilling rig is a small community in itself with up to 200 people working at any one time. Once a shift, usually three weeks, has been completed, the crew leaves by helicopter for Aberdeen airport and another crew is flown in to take its place.

Avonmouth Dock was opened in 1877, and replaced Bristol Docks, six miles up the famous Avon Gorge, as one of Britain's busiest ports. The Royal Edward Dock was opened later and in 1978 The Royal Portbury Dock *(below)* came into operation as the most modern in the group. As with other docks around the coast of Britain, the Port of Bristol, as these docks are collectively known, is in the process of modernisation to cope with the changes that have taken place in the shipping of imports and exports. A wide variety of general cargoes are handled while there are specialist facilities for dry bulk commodities, petroleum products, forest products and export project cargoes. These British-built tractors are assembled at the Royal Portbury Dock prior to being exported to the Middle East.

COASTAL ARCHITECTURE

Britain's coastal architecture presents a richness of buildings and construction that are as varied as the coast they are built upon. Fisherman's cottages, martello towers, piers, sea-front guesthouses and lighthouses represent just a few examples, and are usually part of a fascinating historical story. We can discover resort towns which have become large and crowded whereas before they could be reached by the railways, they were little more than fishing villages; ancient coastal chapels that in spite of falling into dereliction, retain a powerful atmosphere, steeped in folklore; picturesque cobbled streets leading down to harbours surrounded by traditional fishermen's cottages; castles that have protected these shores for 2000 years. Some buildings are unique to a specific town or area of the coast, while others are universal in their appearance. Piers like this one at Hastings, Sussex, were synonomous with a resort's eminence. Many are now in disrepair but others are being restored to their former glory as examples of Britain's coastal heritage.

Lighthouses or beacons in some form have been in existence around the British coast for hundreds of years. But it was not until John Smeaton, a London based clockmaker, built the third Eddystone lighthouse 12½ miles off the Plymouth coast that they could withstand the onslaught of weather and the risk of fire. With a light source of 24 'candles' and visible for five miles it appears feeble when compared to the lighthouse at Trevose Head, Cornwall *(left)* which has the equivalent of 800,000 candela – candlepower – and is visible for over 27 miles. Most lighthouses in England and Wales are administered by Trinity House, whose origins can be traced back to the Middle Ages, and many are open to the public.

The North Foreland lighthouse, Kent *(below left)* has a history that dates back to the fourteenth century. The present lighthouse, warning shipping of the treacherous Goodwin Sands, has gone through many changes. These have included heightening it in 1793 and rendering its flint and brick facing. It was subsequently lowered to its present height of 85 feet but its beam is still visible for over twenty miles.

The lighthouse at Southerness *(below)* stands like a sentinel on the Solway Firth to identify the entrance to the Nith estuary. It has fallen into disuse, and under depressing grey skies and in a desolate landscape its demise reflects the decline of shipping in this area where once schooners sailed in and out of Dumfries to the 'New World.'

The lighthouse standing on South Stack *(right)* which is a small island off Holy Island, is automatically operated.

Clovelly (below) was once an important North Devon fishing port. Now a haven for tourists it has managed to retain the charm that is the epitomy of an English coastal village.

Walking down the steep cobbled and narrow street to the harbour below is like stepping back in time. From its summit the two rows of whitewashed cottages, inn and chapel contrast brilliantly against the blue of Bideford Bay. From spring and throughout the summer these well preserved buildings are bedecked with flowers and shrubs. Cars are banned from Clovelly, but there is a Landrover service that will take those who cannot accommodate the steep climb to and from the harbour. The only transport you are likely to see are the donkeys or the local inhabitants pulling sledges. The Red Lion Hotel overlooks the harbour which prospered in the eighteenth and nineteenth centuries. But the days when herring were caught in vast numbers are long gone, and now the few boats used by local lobster fishermen are outnumbered by pleasure craft.

On a much larger scale but equally as prosperous in the nineteenth century is Aberystwyth (right). Built on the west coast of Wales overlooking Cardigan Bay, Aberystwyth is an important university town. The original college was a splendid Gothic building on the seafront by the pier, but it soon became inadequate and a new college was built on Penglais Hill. This also houses the National Library of Wales which contains the world's largest collection of books relating to Wales or those in the Welsh language. A terrace of well-preserved guest houses and hotels skirt the seafront. Brightly painted, but not garishly so, they contrast spectacularly in the setting sun which they face. A really splendid view over Aberystwyth is obtained from the top of Constitution Hill at the northern end of town. This can be reached by a steep cliff path or alternatively by cable railway.

Many buildings are unique to the coast and the three opposite are an example of Britain's rich maritime history. Although many have outlived their original function their preservation is important as they tell us much about the changing nature of fishing, industry or the defences of these island shores against invasion. The row of wooden weatherboard buildings *(opposite top left)* are yacht stores. Many people mistakenly refer to them as sail lofts but they were built at Tollesbury in Essex to accommodate the gear from racing yachts that used to winter there. They are thought to have been built between 1904-6 and have been renovated and restored by an organisation called Fellowship Afloat.

The sheds used for drying nets and storing fishing tackle *(opposite top right)* are another type of wooden weatherboard building. These are at the east end of the beach at Hastings, Sussex which is still a busy fishing area. Black

tarred, the sheds known locally as 'deezes' are some three stories high and are unique to Hastings. Some of them date from the 17th century but it is thought that the design could be Norse in origin. In fact, Hastings teems with interesting buildings and a disused Victorian chapel set among these sheds is now a fisherman's museum.

The martello tower at Aldeburgh, Suffolk *(opposite below)* was one of a series built in the early 19th century. Erected in haste through fear of invasion by Napoleon and his armies 103 towers were strung out from Aldeburgh to Seaford in Sussex. They were simple but rugged in design and modelled on a fort at Mortella in Corsica which had come under heavy bombardment by the British in 1794. Constructed with thick walls and lookout windows, each one accommodated several men and stores. A cannon was mounted on the roof. The threat of invasion subsided and the towers were never put to the test,

although some were used as observation posts in World War II. Many have fallen into ruins but some, such as the Wish Tower at Eastbourne, Sussex have been turned into museums, while a few others have been converted into very original homes.

Although there is a martello tower at Eastbourne *(above)* it is hard to imagine that it would oppose anything more ferocious than a visiting bowls team. Eastbourne's gentility is reflected in the many dignified red brick Victorian villas that have become a favourite with the retired. Much of the seafront reflects the unhurried air of a population that is satisfied in the knowledge of having 'done its bit.' Playing bowls or listening to a military band on the Grand Parade is a just reward for a generation in the twilight of their days. In having to accommodate this increasingly elderly population, many of the new buildings are apartment blocks which are out of context with the existing architecture.

In complete contrast to Eastbourne, Whitby on the North Yorkshire coast *(preceeding page)* is a robust seafaring town which is anything but retiring. Built on either side of the river Esk, it is overlooked by the ruined abbey to the east and a statue of James Cook to the west. Cook was not born at Whitby but there is much to keep his memory alive and three of the ships, *Endeavour*, *Resolution* and *Adventure*, which took him on his epic voyages around the world were built here. The old town is a maze of narrow winding streets, like Baxtergate and Flowergate, whose pantiled houses are as varied as they are numerous. The west side of Whitby developed later as a resort and is much more formal in its layout with fine terraces of Victorian and Edwardian houses, the most famous being the East Terrace designed by John Dobson in 1848. Many of the shops, especially in Church Street, sell Whitby Jet. Found on the shore locally, Jet is fossilised wood which has undergone a chemical change in stagnant water and has been flattened by enormous pressure. Whitby museum also has many examples of jewellery made from Jet. The harbour entrance is another fine architectural feature. Viewed from the east cliff the two walls that extend either side of the Esk reach out like a giant pincer into the North Sea.

This squat fisherman's house *(top)* in the Orkneys is built for protection against the strong winds. Many Orcadian houses are single storey and you almost feel that they are fixed like limpets to a rock on the seashore.

St Govan's chapel on the South Wales coast *(left bottom)* is situated precariously halfway down a rocky cliff face. Dating from the 13th century, but possibly even earlier, little is known of St Govan from whom this tiny chapel takes its name. The rough rock cell with its stone altar is reached from the cliff top by a steep flight of steps. Tradition says that the empty bell cote once housed a silver bell which was stolen by pirates. Further down towards the sea is a well, now dry, which is also dedicated to St Govan. This was once a place of pilgrimage because the waters were thought to have healing qualities beneficial to cripples or sufferers of eye disease.

The colourful and original doorway of a house *(right)* is in Clovelly whose picturesque cobbled street is described earlier.

The view from Conwy Castle *(below)* toward Conwy Bay shows one of the

many circular towers that dominate the town and quay. Started in the 13th century by Edward 1st it is probably the best preserved of the castles which he

built in North West Wales. As well as the castle, the town is fortified with an equally well-preserved wall with many battlements and gateways. The basic plan of the town, including the castle, town walls, quay and streets was built very quickly and took shape between 1283 and 1287. There are three bridges that cross the River Conwy by the castle. Telford built the first in 1825, a suspension bridge, which is now only used by pedestrians. This was followed by Stephenson's railway bridge in 1848 and finally a road bridge in 1958. From the quay, which reputedly has the smallest house in Britain, measuring only six feet across and 10 feet to the top of its second storey, it is possible to take fishing and pleasure trips which give unrivalled views of the castle. Sea fishing is still an important part of Conwy's economy, with catches of plaice, whiting, mackerel and dabs being landed but gone are the days of a flourishing mussel industry which reached its peak in the mid-nineteenth century when up to eight hundred bags a week were being sent to markets the length and breadth of the country.

Tenby harbour *(above)* is overlooked by an array of Georgian and Regency buildings and must rank as one of the most picturesque in South Wales. Developed as a resort in the early nineteenth century Tenby soon became favoured by the Victorians not just as a summer resort between June and late September but, because of the mild climate, a winter one too. Sir William Paxton built Laston House for seawater baths in 1811 and soon the now familiar structures flourished as guest houses. These buildings represent how we see Tenby today but its history goes back much further and there has probably been a town or settlement on the site since before the ninth century. The remains of the present castle and walls were begun in the twelfth and completed in the fourteenth. Virtually impregnable until the onslaught of Cromwell's firepower in 1644, the walls are the most intact of any from that period surviving in South Wales, and include the famous five-arched south gateway. Other indications of Tenby's prosperity can be seen by the size and splendour of the parish church of St Mary and the magnificent Tudor Merchant's House on Quay Hill. Probably built in the late fifteenth century it is now owned by the National Trust. Tenby is still an important resort town and has four sandy beaches. The South Beach at one and a half miles in length is the largest,

fact the largest town on the north west coast of Scotland. It has also developed into the most important fishing port on the west coast. Ullapool was planned by Thomas Telford and a short walk through its streets confirms that the grid design was strictly adhered to. It was in 1788 that the British Fisheries Society decided to establish a fishing station here as a base from which to exploit the rich herring shoals from the nearby seas of northern Britain. Although its prosperity subsequently declined as a result of over-fishing, Ullapool is now very firmly back on the map and many of the original buildings still survive. These include the Arch Inn and the old herring-curing factory which has now been made into a small museum, as well as the fisherman's cottages along Shore Street. Many of these buildings are now guest houses or hotels like the Old Bank House in Argyle Street whose history typifies their changing role. In fact tourism is now as important to Ullapool as fishing, and with the development of off-shore oil exploration it may not be an exaggeration to predict that Ullapool could become the Aberdeen of the west coast.

and Tenby's bustling and colourful streets are full of restaurants, especially those serving locally caught fish.

Seen from the main road in the early morning light *(right)* Ullapool's sea front terrace of whitewashed buildings reflect serenely in the waters of Loch Broom. From this distance it is hard to imagine that Ullapool's quayside is teeming with the kind of activity usually associated with far larger ports. With a population of some 1100 inhabitants Ullapool is in

This row of cottages *(left)* are typical of the buildings of Shieldaig, a small village on Scotland's north west coast. Lit by a shaft of brilliant sunlight they contrast dramatically with the dark water of Loch Shieldaig.

Dartmouth *(below)* has a long tradition as a seafaring town and many of the buildings are outstanding examples of fine architecture. The colonnaded seventeenth century Butterwalk was damaged by bombing in World War II but has been sympathetically restored and houses one of Dartmouth's museums. Baynard's Cove has a picturesque cobbled quay and a fine row of old houses including the Customs House of 1739. On the hill above Dartmouth stands the Royal Naval College which was built in 1905 to replace the Britannia training ship. Dartmouth Castle was one of the first designed to accommodate cannons and was built with seven. The houses of Kingswear can be seen across the River Dart through a flotilla of small craft and invariably a visiting warship. This is the southern terminus of the Dart Valley Railway, which was opened in 1864. As well as running steam trains through attractive countryside it has some finely preserved stations.

Mevagissey in Cornwall *(right)* is a typical Cornish fishing village, built around the harbour. Narrow streets rise steeply from the quayside and are usually thronged with tourists in the summer.

FISHING COMMUNITIES

Many of today's fishing communities can be traced back to as early as Roman times, and in certain areas the type of fishing carried out today has changed little since those times. But while tradition plays an important part in the life of a fisherman and his community, recent changes are having quite radical and in many opinions damaging effects on fishing and fish stocks. The use of huge factory ships, known as Klondikers on the north west coast of Scotland, have decimated certain shoals of fish.

Mevagissey in Cornwall is now just a shadow of the bustling fishing village that it used to be, and where mackerel fishing provided a livelihood for many, now only a few boats are active. Fish stocks have also been depleted by the consequences of industrial pollution. In Scotland, higher wages have lured many fishermen to work on the North Sea oil rigs or in related industries. Nevertheless fishing continues, and the concept of Britain without its fishing industry seems inconceivable.

The picture of tangled fishing nets at Newlyn harbour in Cornwall *(left)* could be seen at any quayside where fishermen regularly land their catch. Bringing the fish to market is the culmination of a night's work that often continues immediately with the preparations for the next trip. As well as sorting nets, work may have to be done to the ships and their equipment. The welder *(below)* is repairing a trawl door that has been broken by the buffeting it has received in the sea as it holds the trawl net open. With more of the larger ships being made of steel instead of wood, the call for ancillary craftsmen has increased.

Hastings *(right)* still has an active fishing industry although many boats have disappeared. Those that remain can be seen winched up onto the beach known as The Stade. Fresh fish can be bought direct from the boats or from several nearby stalls. Many fishing boats at Hastings are local craft called Luggers, recognisable for their high sterns and robust build. Inshore fishing boats vary from one another according to where they are based. The Coble is as familiar to the north east as the Lugger is to Hastings. Other types of boats include Dogger, Hooker, and Drifter.

The fisherman (below) is an example of such a dying breed. All his life he has worked at Goldcliff, Gwent, in the Severn estuary, catching salmon. These swim down the Severn and Wye rivers into the estuary. A wooden frame is stretched along the low-lying shore into the sea. This holds the special tapering baskets known as 'putchers.' The salmon swim into these but are unable to pass through, and as it is impossible for the fish to turn round they simply drown. During the season, which lasts from April 15th until August 15th, some 2000 putchers are laid down, and salmon up to 30 pounds in weight are caught. In the off-season period there is work to be done repairing the putchers or constructing new ones. These used to be made of wickerwork, but are now made with metal wire. It is likely that this fisherman is the last to be practising his special skill, and this activity will cease in the near future when he finally retires.

The characters who catch the fish are as varied as the coast of Britain. Hands and faces weathered by wind and sea bear testament to rugged lives spent at the mercy of the elements. Early in the morning when the boats come in, or later at the local pub, it is difficult to miss the good-humoured camaraderie of a group of sea-dogs. Many speak loudly, wise-cracking and holding court. Others are quieter, possibly older but wiser in the ways of the sea. All will have their own share of sea stories, both funny and sad. Some have had to change from traditional fishing such as for mackerel, to catching lobster or crab, as the larger boats and factory ships have decimated the shoals found in local waters. Mevagissey for example, is a shadow of its former character, with several smaller boats now organising fishing trips for holidaymakers as a way of eeking out a living. Many other fishermen are becoming the last in a particular line of fishing that demands skills only they possess.

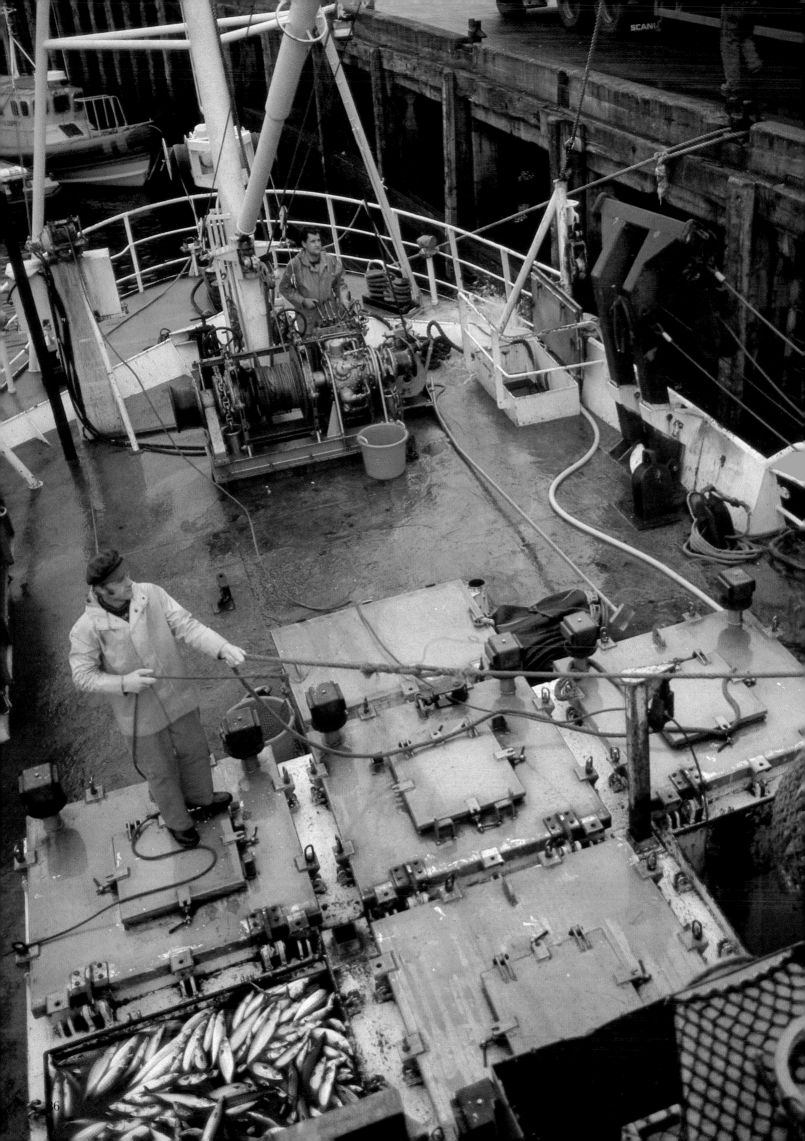

Ullapool *(previous page and left)* is now the premier fishing port on the west coast of Scotland. From the hills that slope down to Loch Broom it is possible to look over the town and harbour to the sea beyond. At the entrance to the loch, 20 to 30 fishing vessels and factory ships anchor in the sheltered waters. As soon as one ship has disgorged its catch at the quayside, another is ready to replace it. When fishing is plentiful, this process continues day and night, to the annoyance of some of the local residents. Once a ship has berthed, its haul of 150 to 200 tons of fish is rapidly unloaded from the large chambers below deck. This is winched out and packed with ice into crates to be loaded directly onto juggernaut lorries. A fleet of these stand constantly at the ready on the quayside. Rumbling out of Ullapool, they transport their loads either to market, or more likely to another dock where they will end up in the countries of the Eastern Bloc. The crew of these ships will probably return at the same time

next day with an equally large catch. Since they only have a limited time on shore, they monopolise the telephone boxes on the quay, making hurried calls to wives and girlfriends for news and reassurance. A large amount of money can be earned chasing the shoals down the west coast but this is offset by the anxiety and discontent that may result within the family through such long absences.

Lifeboats are manned by volunteers, many of whom are fishermen. The lifeboat *(below)* is the Penlee Lifeboat, named the *Mabel Alice*. On December 19th 1981 its predecessor made a fatal rescue attempt in which eight members of the crew perished. It is an Arun Class lifeboat, one of the Royal National Lifeboat Institution's 'Fast Afloat Boats' (FABS) that lie permanently afloat in harbours. With a special semi-planing hull form, it is twice as fast as earlier classes of lifeboats, able to reach a speed of 18 knots. Other lifeboats fitted with displacement hulls and protected

propellers in tunnels can only do a speed of eight to nine knots. There are two survivors cabins below deck containing rescue equipment including first aid gear, stretchers, emergency rations and blankets. The wheelhouse is fitted with seats having safety belts and arm-rests, one for each member of the crew. There are special positions for the coxswain, navigator, radio operator, mechanic and crew members, and provision for a doctor. The RNLI was founded in 1824 and is responsible for saving over 110,000 lives. The average number of launches per year has now reached 3000 or approximately eight every day of the year. It is essentially a voluntary service and as such relies entirely on contributions from the general public, requiring in the region of £19 million a year to maintain the standard of its present activities.

Mallaig *(above)* is a fishing village that grew with the coming of the railways. Built in 1901, the extension of the West Highland Railway was to transform Mallaig from a poor crofting settlement into one of West Scotland's busiest fishing ports. Within a couple of years ships from the east coast of Scotland that fished the waters of the Inner Hebrides started to land their catches there. Before long, these fishermen began to make their homes in Mallaig and gradually it became the most important port on this coast. It is only recently that it has lost this position to Ullapool. Shellfish predominates the fishing at Mallaig, and the Saturday morning auctions on the quayside often deal with as many as 10,000 pounds of lobsters. As well as fishing, Mallaig is famous for the picturesque road that connects it with Fort William, which is known as 'The Road to the Isles.'

capture a small fort that defended the harbour. With the decline of the coal trade, the prosperity of the port has dwindled and only a handful of the original buildings remain. Meanwhile, fishing on a small-scale continues and fresh fish can be bought on the quayside.

Carnarfon Castle *(below)* presents a dramatic backdrop to the quayside lined with berthed fishing vessels. Although it is not a major fishing port, the quay and the small dock on the northern side of the town are still active. The castle was one of the most powerful built by Edward I in the 13th century, and is situated on the Menai Strait in North Wales. In 1301, Edward crowned his son as Prince of Wales, and ever since that time, this title has been conferred on the male Heir Apparent. Prince Charles' Investiture was held there in 1969. The boats on the quay provide holiday visitors with both pleasure and fishing trips. The main catch in this area consists of bass and tope. Local fishermen have a mine of information to impart, and as with other fishing ports, many are willing to take one or two people along, which is the best way to see commercial fishing in action.

Whitehaven *(left)* is an example of a small coastal village that has seen prosperity and decline but throughout its history has retained its links with fishing. In the late 16th century Whitehaven consisted of just six fisherman's cottages. In 1634, Christopher Lowther built a small pier to serve this tiny community. For the next two hundred years successive generations of Lowthers turned Whitehaven into a major port and industrial town. Sir John Lowther laid out the town using a grid design and Whitehaven developed as a port for shipbuilding and the export of coal. By the 18th century, during the American War of Independence, its emminence was such that the Scots-born American naval commander John Paul Jones mounted an attack on it in 1778. His attempt to set fire to the merchant fleet failed, although he did manage to

Newlyn *(above)* is Cornwall's largest and most important fishing port. The majority of Cornwall's ports have experienced a dramatic decline in the fishing industry, but Newlyn has managed to remain buoyant. On most days a throng of vessels of every size can be seen unloading their catches ready to be sold at the quayside market. This market *(opposite top)* bears many reminders of turbulent times in the past. In the late 19th century for example, armed police had to break up a riot when local fishermen objected to trawlers from the east coast fishing on Sundays. Today discontent is still found among some of the local fishermen, many of whom

blame large modern boats from the Scottish coast for over-fishing and depleting the stocks of mackerel. This has caused a considerable number to abandon mackerel fishing and concentrate on catching crab and lobster in the summer months, and fishing for sea bass by hand in December and January. It is an unstable way of earning a living, which is reflected in the fact that many have to claim unemployment benefit until the crab and lobster season begins again.

Smoking fish *(right)* is a tradition that far from declining, is enjoying a steadily growing market. This method is not to be confused with the poor imitations

claiming to be smoked fish seen on many supermarket shelves which are simply dyed and have never seen the inside of a smokehouse. An authentically smoked kipper, like these in Whitby, make for a memorable breakfast. Kippers are in fact herrings, which before they are smoked are split open and then soaked in brine. Once this process is complete they are attached to metal rods and suspended in the smokehouse. This is a building of simple construction, having one tall chimney towering above its roof. A fire is lit on the concrete floor, and it is this fire that kippers the herring. The wood used is oak, although in different areas a mix may be used to give a

distinctive flavour. The walls inside the smokehouse are shiny black from the tarry deposits built up over many years of smoking. The aim is to have as much smoke as possible so the fire smoulders without a flame. With no means of escape except the chimney, the smoke is drawn up from the floor to the herrings suspended above. The fire needs constant attention to maintain enough smoke. The process takes many hours before the fish take on their characteristic colour and flavour.

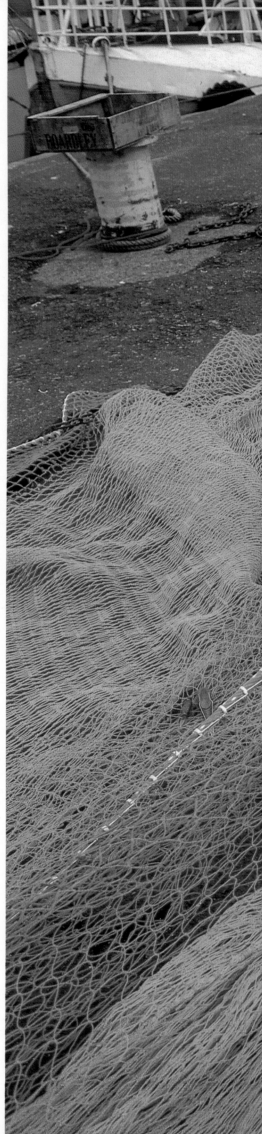

Large-scale fishing and trawling has become very sophisticated with the development of sonor equipment and other technology, but for the traditional small fisherman it is almost as difficult as it ever was. Apart from the addition of radar, most still rely on well-used equipment and large nets, which need constant checking and maintenance, as seen here at Newlyn *(below)* and Troon in south west Scotland *(right)*.

The Whitby fisherman *(above)* has just unloaded his boat and is about to snatch a bit of time at home before setting out on the next trip. Dependence on the weather and the speed of making a catch makes the fisherman's work hard and unpredictable. He may be out all times of the day or night and family life is fitted in between. Being married to a fisherman can be a lonely and anxious life. There is always a fear at the back of women's minds as they kiss their husbands goodbye that some unforeseen accident could happen. Consequently, there is a strong sense of solidarity and support among fishermen and their wives within traditional fishing communities. Whatever improvements are made to the boats, they are still subject to the whims of the elements, and the sea has always claimed its share of lives. Bits of old wrecks that emerge off the coast at low tide provide a constant reminder that this kind of life always contains a lurking element of danger. The many Fishermen's or Seamen's Museums such as in Whitby, Hastings, and Southwold in Suffolk provide moving testimony of the lives of fishing communities over the last few centuries. However, there can be great satisfaction in working outdoors, challenging the elements and bringing home the day's catch instead of being confined to a routine indoor job in an office or factory.

The crab pots *(left)* at Lulworth Cove, Dorset are stacked by the slipway. October marks the end of the season and they will not be required again until late next spring. Similarly, at this time boats and other equipment will be brought ashore to be repaired or stored.

Many of the boats at Whitby *(below)* will also be laid up for the winter and with each passing year many fishermen will not return to the sea as making a living with a small boat becomes more difficult. Meanwhile, fishing for pleasure continues in popularity, evidenced by the lines of optimistic fishermen of all ages who line the harbour quays, as in Mevagissey *(right)*. Some of the luckier ones will catch the elusive mackerel, but most will hook the long, spindly, and unappetizing garfish.

Index

The photographs were taken by the author, who thanks Sue Sharpe for her invaluable assistance throughout the preparation of this book.